DOUNE CASTLE

Text by J. K. Anderson, models by Nick Taylor

"Forth," as the saying goes, "bridles the wild Highlandman," but any ruler of the Lowlands of Scotland who wished to secure the line of the River Forth was well advised to push his defences out to the edge of the hills beyond. Doune is an advanced post in the defence of this line, guarding the road that runs up the River Teith into the Trossachs and so through "bonny Strathyre" into the heart of the Highlands. A second road, skirting the edge of the Highlands from south-west to north-east and linking the ancient cities of Glasgow and Perth, also passed through Doune, so that, though most modern traffic flows by other routes, the Bridge of Doune was once a major link in the communications of Central Scotland, and the castle of strategic importance.

The site, though not spectacular, is naturally strong — a low hill lying in the tongue of land between the left bank of the Teith and its tributary, the Ardoch Water, which comes down out of the moorlands to the north. What Celtic chieftain's "dun," or stronghold, gave its name to the place we do not know; the traces of earthworks that can still be seen outside the present castle may be prehistoric. These include the deep ditch that guards the approach to the castle from the north (the side on which it is not protected by the streams), though no doubt this ditch was enlarged when the castle was built. The top of the hill has been levelled to form a platform on which the castle stands, and its sides artificially sloped so that the attackers could not reach the foot of the walls without climbing a steep bank.

Doune was built about two hundred years after Château Gaillard*, in the late fourteenth century. It uses some of the ideas that Richard Coeur de Lion built into his great castle, such as an outward batter at the foot of the wall: this made it thicker while at the same time eliminating the "dead angle" that could not be covered by fire, and caused missiles dropped from the ramparts to spatter outwards in the attacker's faces. But the overall plan shows a complete change in military thinking. At Gaillard the strongest part of the castle, the great donjon, was only reached after three successive outer lines of defence had been forced. It was planned as a "keep," where the defenders could make a last stand. But in practice that last stand was not made — and the same thing happened at other castles whose defences were planned in the same way. The door of the "keep" was too narrow and inaccessible for the defenders to scramble into it with their enemies at their heels when the rest of the castle was stormed.

At Doune the stronger part of the castle was placed where the main force of the enemy's attack was likely to come. And in other ways its arrangements show that the builder was a very different man from King Richard, and living in a different age.

Robert, Duke of Albany was the brother of King Robert III of Scotland. It seems strange that both brothers were called "Robert." The reason is that the older was christened "John," but when he came to the throne men said that John Balliol in Scotland, King John of England and King John of France, who was captured at Poitiers by the Black Prince, had all been unlucky. So they changed his name to Robert, after his great ancestor Robert the Bruce. But poor "Robert III" did not change his luck with his name. He had been lamed by the kick of a horse when he was still a boy, and could never lead his armies in battle. He was a well-meaning and religious man, but the times called for a strong soldier.

For a century, ever since King Edward I of England had unjustly tried to make himself lord of Scotland, there had been almost continuous war between the kingdoms —

> "What weenit the King of England
> Sae soon to have won Scotland?"

Although the Scots kept their freedom, the wars had torn the kingdom in pieces. The Highland clans fought one another and the representatives of the king, whom they mocked as "King of Fife and Lothian" — that is, of no more of Scotland than could be seen from Edin-

---

*Château Gaillard is described in Bellerophon Books' *CASTLES — to cut out* (Book I).

burgh Castle. In the Lowlands, the great lords raised bands of mercenary ruffians, as well as their own tenants, and in their search for plunder were as ready to harry each other's lands as to ride

"Into England, to drive a prey."

Of them all, the Duke of Albany was the strongest and craftiest. Perhaps he planned to seize the throne for himself; at all events, he took advantage of the foolish misbehaviour of the heir to the throne, his nephew David, Duke of Rothesay, had him arrested on a warrant from the King, and left him to starve to death in prison. But the king still had one son left, Prince James, a child of nine. In 1405, three years after his brother's death, he was sent to France to be brought up at the French King's court. But, although there was peace between Scotland and England at the time, the prince's ship was seized on the high seas by the English, and King Henry of England refused to let the boy go, saying that he could be taught as easily in England as in France. The news of his son's capture was brought to poor old King Robert as he sat at supper. He fell forward senseless, and, not long after, died.

Now Robert of Albany was Regent of Scotland in his nephew's name, and he was in no hurry to bring King James back home. So Robert ruled in Scotland until he died in 1420, at the age of more than eighty, and his son Murdoch became Regent after him. But so far from ruling the kingdom, Murdoch could not even control his own children. He had a favourite falcon which his oldest son wanted. When Murdoch refused to give it to him, the boy snatched it off his father's wrist and wrung its neck. "I cannot govern you," said Murdoch, "but now I will bring home one whom we must all obey." So he sent ambassadors into England, and in 1424 James was brought back. The English could not demand a ransom for him, since he had been captured in peace-time, but instead they sent a large bill for his education.

Now Murdoch and his son were called to account for all that they had done during the King's captivity, and their heads were cut off at Stirling. As they stood on the Heading Hill, in front of the castle, they could see in the distance the towers of the fortress that Duke Robert had built at Doune.

The castle of Doune was a favourite residence of Duke Robert from 1401 onwards. (It certainly was not built during Murdoch's short regency, as some people have thought.) The castle's plan shows changes not only in the theory of defence, but in the whole concept of feudalism, by which land was held in return for military service. No longer would a great lord require his own knights to garrison his fortresses by serving as "castle guard" for part of each year. Instead, he would excuse them their service in return for a cash payment, with which he would hire mercenaries. Although the mercenaries were efficient professionals and permanently on duty, they were not be trusted like the lord's own men, and this distrust is reflected in the plan of Doune.

The most impressive part of the castle is a great rectangular tower block, nearly a hundred feet high and containing four stories and a garret. Through this block passes a vaulted passage fifty feet long leading into the castle's courtyard. Besides serving as a gatehouse, this block contained the actual residence of the dukes.

Its most exposed corner, the north-east, on the left as one approaches the gate, was strengthened by a projecting round tower of five stories, rising the full height of the block, and round the corner on the east side there is a rectangular projection on top of which was a platform where beacons could be lighted to raise the alarm.

The rooms on the ground floor include, on the right of the entrance passage as one goes in, a guard room and behind it a prison. On the left are store rooms, and, inside the round tower, a well. Stores and water could be drawn up into the rooms above through trapdoors, but there was no regular access to the upper floors from this basement.

To reach the upper floors, one must go the whole length of the entrance passage into the courtyard, passing first great double doors, then a portcullis, then a "yett," a special feature of Scottish castles. This is a double door, each of whose leaves is a grating made of thick iron bars, vertical and horizontal, cunningly meshed together. Finally, at the end of the passage is another double door, facing in the opposite direction, towards the inner court.

The open-air stairway to the next floor is now on one's right. It is screened by a high stone wall, and leads to an arched doorway through which one enters the "Lord's Hall," a huge room, taking up the whole of that floor and covered by a stone barrel-vault more than twenty feet high. At the east end, where the Duke's own high table must have been placed, is a fine stone fireplace, and on its right side a window, opening from a deep recess in the thickness of the wall. A larger recess in the north wall is lighted by another window. It is directly over the outer end of the entrance passage, and contained the machinery for raising and lowering the portcullis. So, from the Lord's Hall it was possible to control everybody who went in or out of the main gate. On the south side of the hall is a small vaulted chamber, reached from the hall by a passage in the thickness of the wall. This has one window looking into the hall, and another towards the court, and from here the duke's steward will have kept an eye on what went on in the castle.

The duke's own private room was in the round tower, opening off the north-west corner of the hall. A hole in the floor of this room gives access to the well, and it also has two small windows, its own fireplace, and a "garderobe" or privy in one corner. Of course, this well was not the main water-supply. Most of the people in the castle would use the great well in the middle of the court.

Spiral stone staircases, set in the thickness of the walls, lead from the north-east and north-west corners of the hall to the "solar" — the "sun-room" or family living-room which occupies the next floor — and the bedrooms on the floors above. Only the most important people had bedrooms; lesser folk will have slept on the rushes that covered the floor of the hall.

A lower block, with a ridged roof running east and west, completes the north side of the castle. Although this is built directly next to the gatehouse tower, the wall between is thick, and there were originally no doors through it, though one has been opened in modern times. This second block contains the "Retainers' Hall," the accommodation for the mercenary garrison. It was because they could be trusted no further than the length of their pay-master's purse that they were given no direct access to the great tower, and arrangements were made to close the entrance passage against the inner court if need arose.

The "Retainers' Hall" stands above three vaulted cellars, each with its own door into the court. It is reached by an outside staircase in the north-west corner of the court. It is even larger than the "Lord's Hall" — sixty-seven feet from west to east and twenty-seven from north to south. It is not vaulted, and its ancient timber roof has perished. But the castle was carefully restored in the 1880's, and a new roof was built, copying the form of the old one.

The west end of this hall was apparently cut off by a wooden screen, behind which were a pantry and a buttery for serving food and drink. There is a stair going down to the cellar below, which was probably the wine-cellar. Above the screen was a minstrels' gallery, from which musicians would entertain banqueters in the hall below. At the south-west corner a door leads through an antechamber into the kitchen, which is housed in another massive stone tower.

The kitchen can also be reached by its own open-air staircase, on the west side of the court, at whose foot a small postern, or side-gate, leads through the wall. This could have been used in peace-time as a "servants' entrance" for bringing in supplies to be housed in the great vaulted cellars on the ground floor of the Kitchen Tower and in war to allow the garrison to sally out unexpectedly.

continued

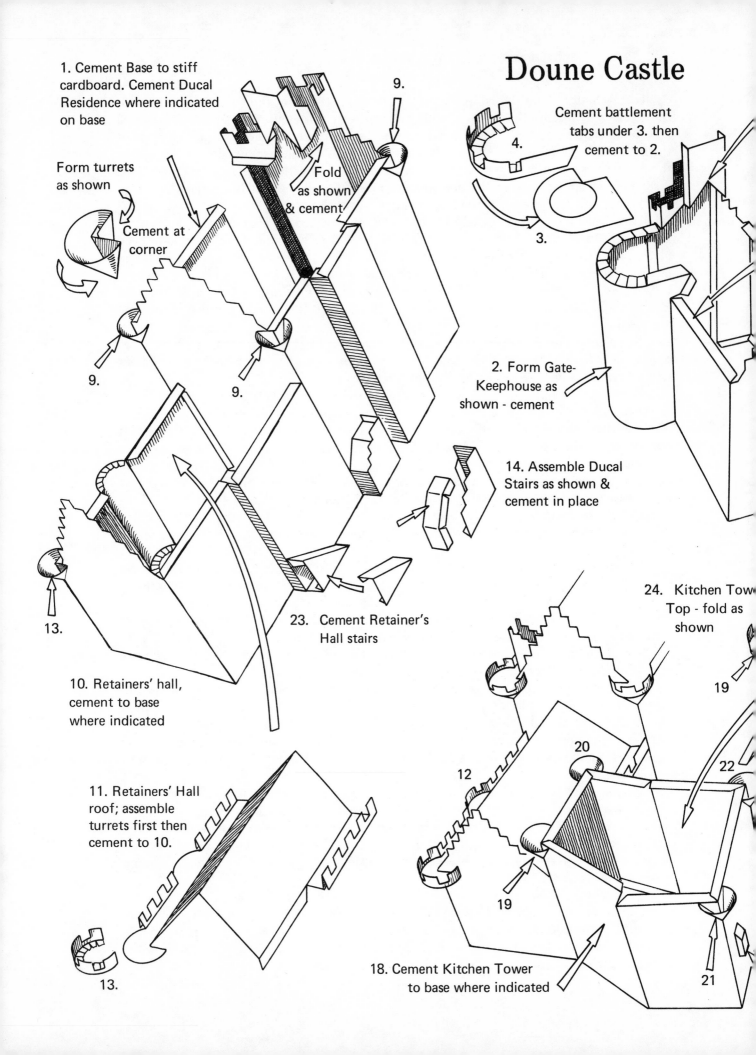

Doune Castle

1. Cement Base to stiff cardboard. Cement Ducal Residence where indicated on base

Form turrets as shown

Cement at corner

Fold as shown & cement

9.

9.

9.

13.

Cement battlement tabs under 3. then cement to 2.

4.

3.

2. Form Gate-Keephouse as shown - cement

14. Assemble Ducal Stairs as shown & cement in place

23. Cement Retainer's Hall stairs

10. Retainers' hall, cement to base where indicated

11. Retainers' Hall roof; assemble turrets first then cement to 10.

13.

24. Kitchen Tower Top - fold as shown

19

12

20

22

19

18. Cement Kitchen Tower to base where indicated

21

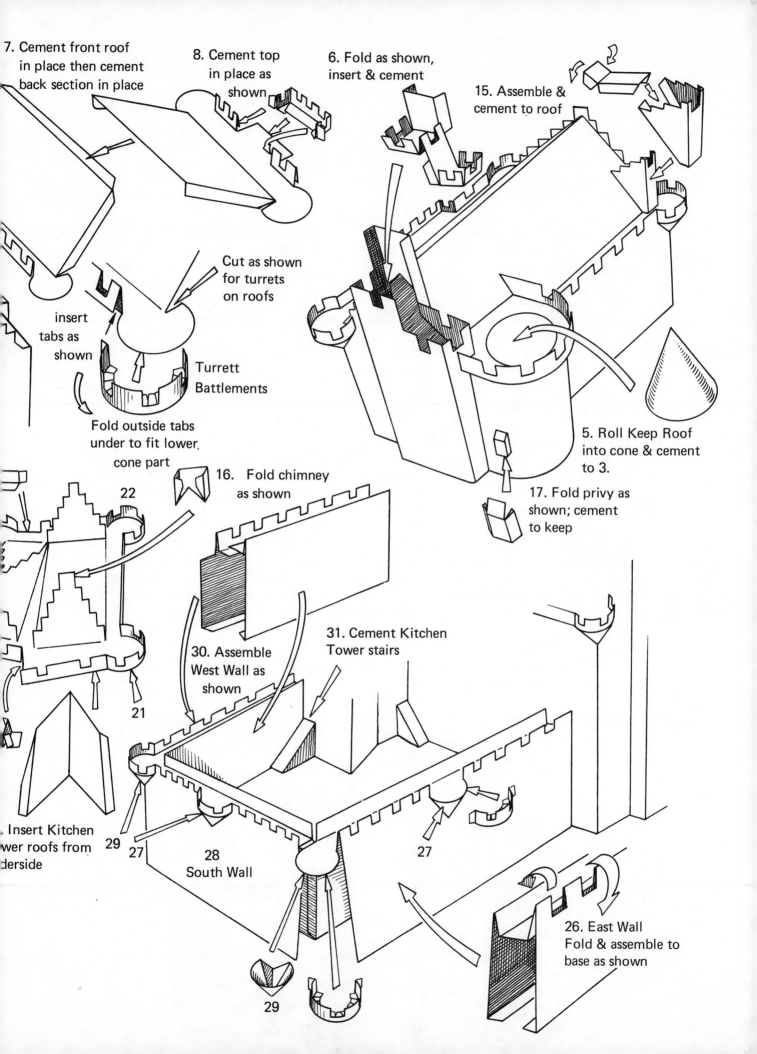

7. Cement front roof in place then cement back section in place

8. Cement top in place as shown

6. Fold as shown, insert & cement

15. Assemble & cement to roof

insert tabs as shown

Cut as shown for turrets on roofs

Turrett Battlements

Fold outside tabs under to fit lower cone part

5. Roll Keep Roof into cone & cement to 3.

17. Fold privy as shown; cement to keep

22

16. Fold chimney as shown

21

30. Assemble West Wall as shown

31. Cement Kitchen Tower stairs

Insert Kitchen Tower roofs from underside

29

27

28 South Wall

27

29

26. East Wall Fold & assemble to base as shown

The kitchen itself occupies one whole floor of its tower. It has a fireproof stone vault, and right across its west end stretches a low arch, eighteen feet wide, which forms the entrance to the huge fireplace. If one stands in the fireplace and looks up, one can see how the chimney narrows to a small patch of sky far above.

From the antechamber between the kitchen and the hall a spiral staircase leads to a suite of apartments at the top of the Kitchen Tower. One might have expected servants' quarters here; but in fact these handsome rooms are the principal guest-chambers of the castle — well heated by the warmth from the kitchen and its chimney, protected from fire by the vault below, and remote from the Duke's own quarters so that he would be safe from the treachery of his guests.

A high curtain wall, forming an irregular quadrilateral, runs round the remaining sides of the court. There is a rampart walk, protected by battlements, round the top, and at the corners and the middle of the sides small bartizans, or turrets, are carried out on corbels so that the defenders could cover the face of the wall with flanking fire.

Two handsome Gothic windows in the south curtain suggest that some important building was planned here — perhaps a chapel for the garrison; there was a small private chapel on the south side of the solar above the "Lord's Hall." But this side of the court was left unfinished at the fall of the Dukes of Albany.

After Murdoch's death, the castle was seized by the king, and entrusted on behalf of the Crown to a keeper. Since the time of Mary Queen of Scots, the keepers have been the Earls of Moray, whose ancestor, Sir James Stewart, a descendant of the Dukes of Albany, married the daughter of Queen Mary's half-brother, the Earl of Moray who acted as Regent for her young son James VI. Mary herself visited Doune more than once, and the guest-rooms in the Kitchen Tower are still known as "Queen Mary's Apartments."

Doune last played a part in history in 1746, when Prince Charles Edward made the castle his headquarters during his unsuccessful siege of Stirling. In a corner of the kitchen are the remains of the oven where his garrison, whose resources were insufficient for the great fireplace, cooked their rations. In Queen Mary's Apartments above were held prisoners taken at the victory of Falkirk, one of whom, John Home, later to become famous as a tragic poet, escaped with several of his friends down a rope of knotted sheets lowered from the rampart walk. (Unfortunately, the fifth to descend was overweight; the rope broke and the two men who tried to follow were injured, one of them fatally.)

Sir Walter Scott used these events in his romance of Waverley. But perhaps Doune is best known today through the tag-end of a lament for a four-hundred-year-old tragedy —

Lang may his lady
Look ower the Castle Doune
Ere she see the Earle of Moray
Comes sounding through the toun.

Doune Castle

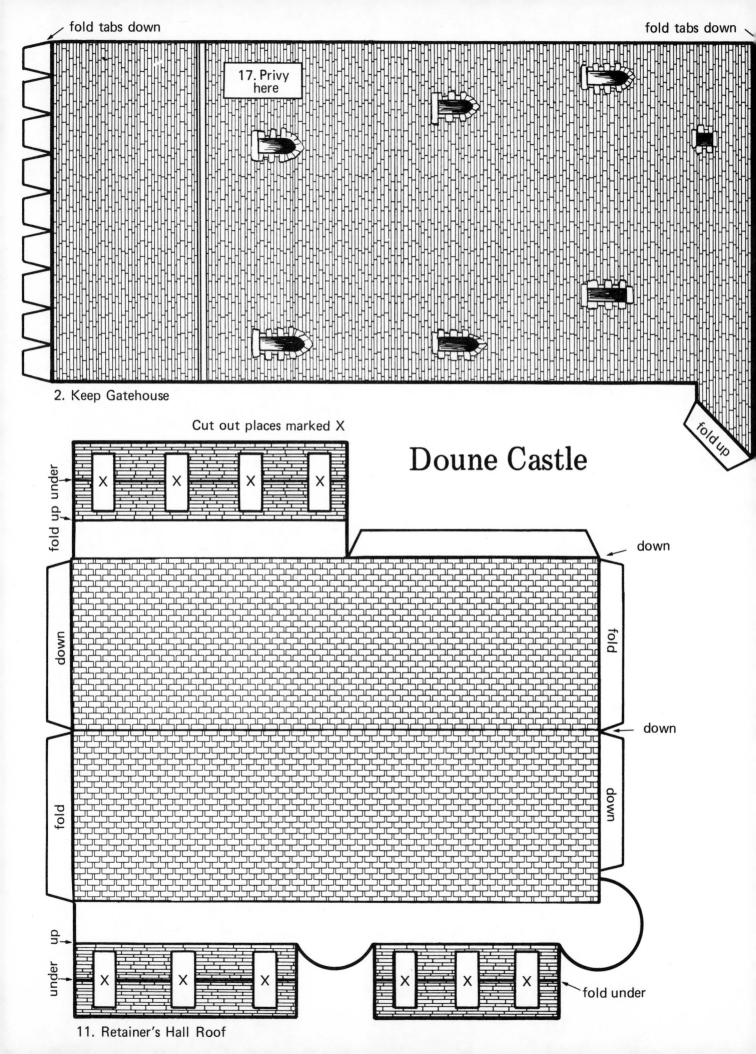

fold tabs down

fold tabs down

17. Privy
here

2. Keep Gatehouse

fold up

Cut out places marked X

Doune Castle

fold up under

X   X   X   X

fold up under

down

down

fold

down

fold

down

up

under

X   X   X

X   X   X

fold under

11. Retainer's Hall Roof

Doune Castle

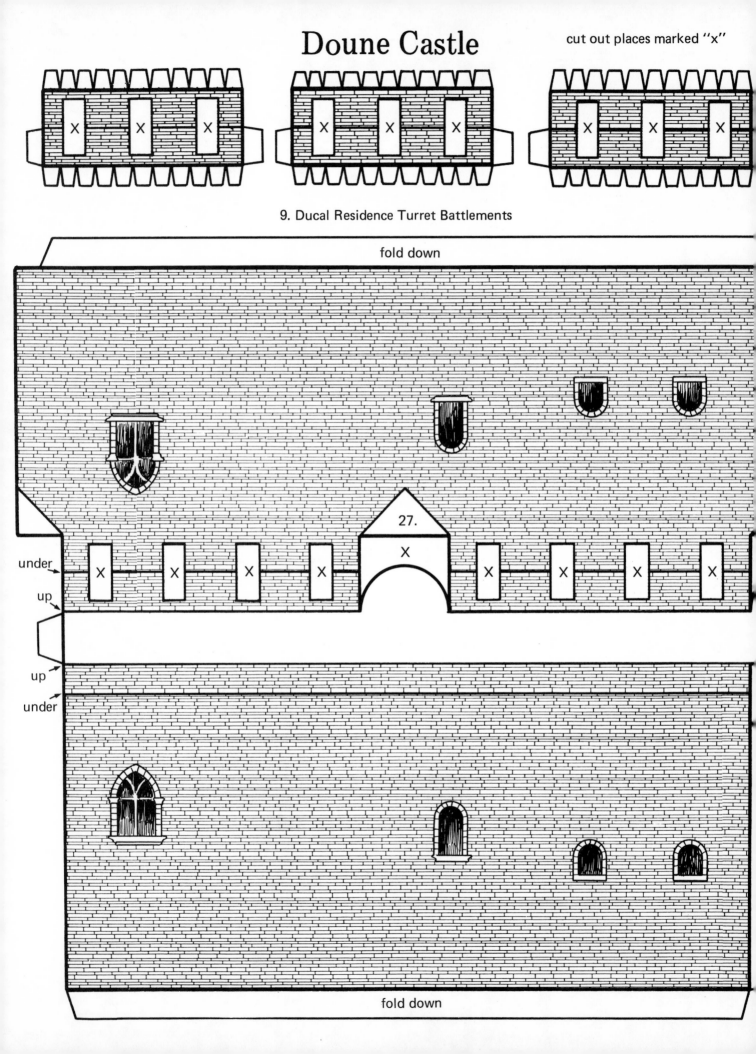

9. Ducal Residence Turret Battlements

fold down

27.

X

under

up

up

under

fold down

Doune Castle

Cut out areas market "x"

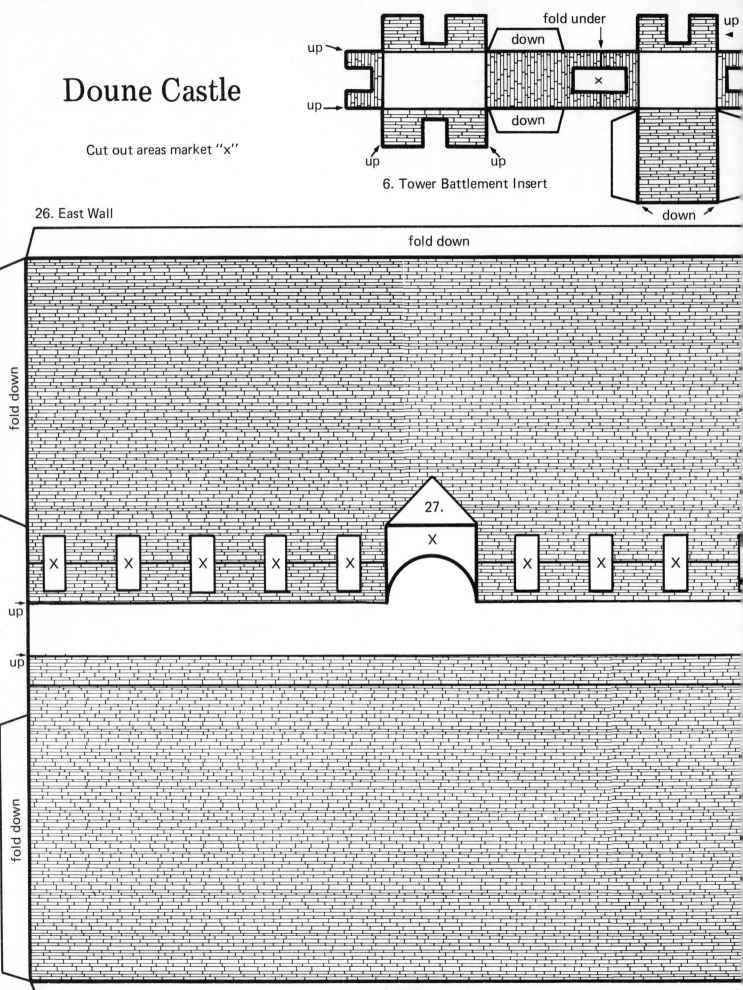

6. Tower Battlement Insert

26. East Wall

27.

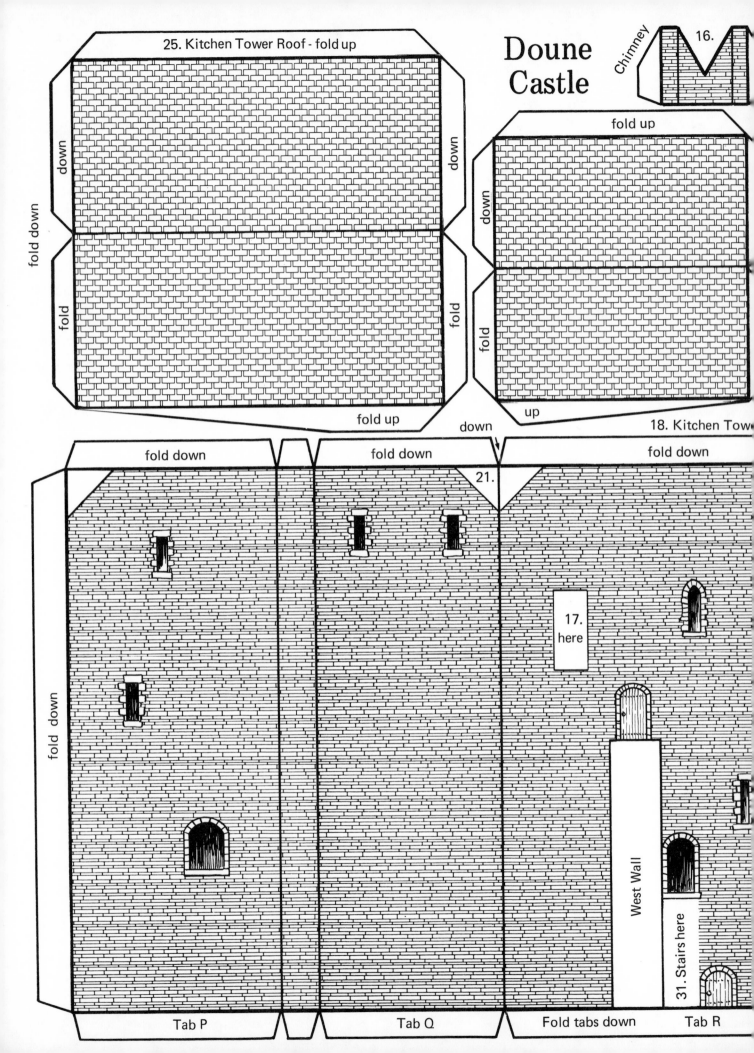

25. Kitchen Tower Roof - fold up

Doune Castle

Chimney   16.

fold up

fold down

down

fold

down

fold

down

up

fold up

down

18. Kitchen Tow

fold down

fold down

21.

fold down

fold down

17.
here

West Wall

31. Stairs here

Tab P

Tab Q

Fold tabs down

Tab R

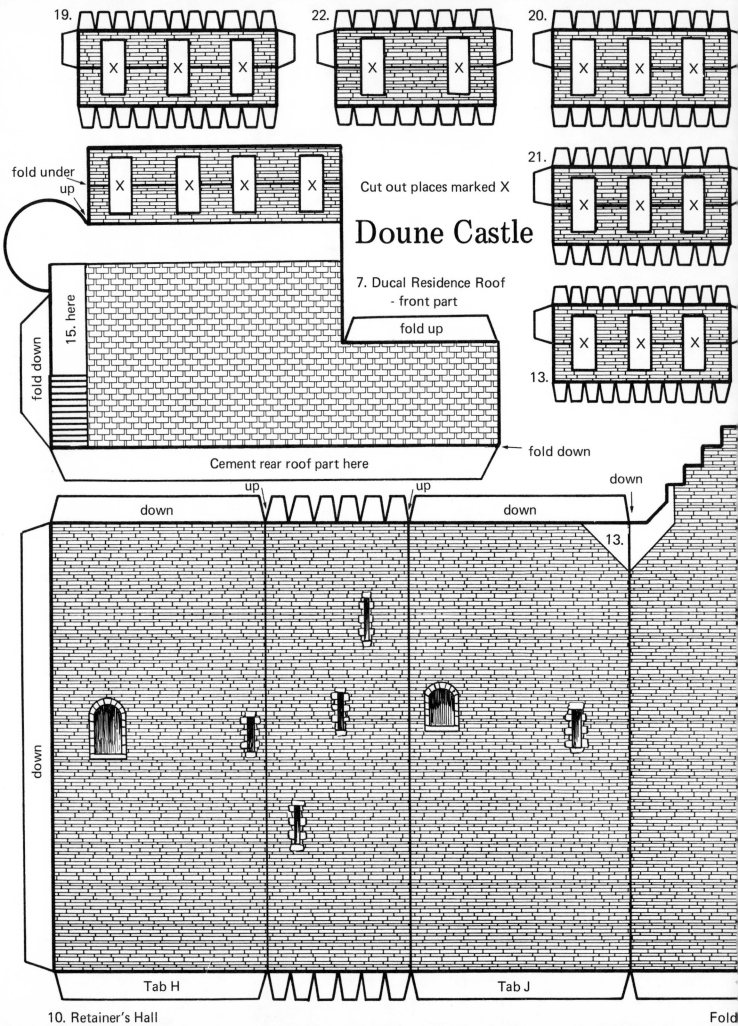

19.

22.

20.

21.

13.

Cut out places marked X

Doune Castle

7. Ducal Residence Roof
   - front part

fold under
up

15. here

fold down

fold up

Cement rear roof part here

fold down

down

down

up

up

down

13.

down

Tab H

Tab J

10. Retainer's Hall

Fold

Doune Castle

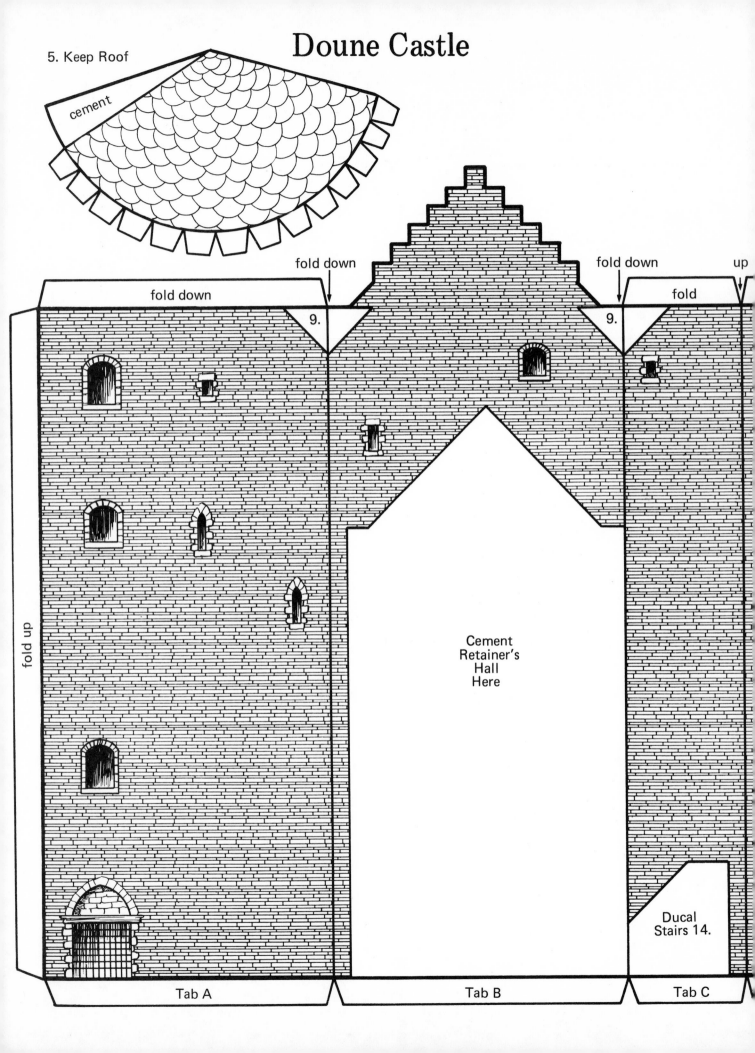

5. Keep Roof

cement

fold down

fold down

up

fold down

fold

9.

9.

fold up

Cement
Retainer's
Hall
Here

Ducal
Stairs 14.

Tab A

Tab B

Tab C

Doune Castle

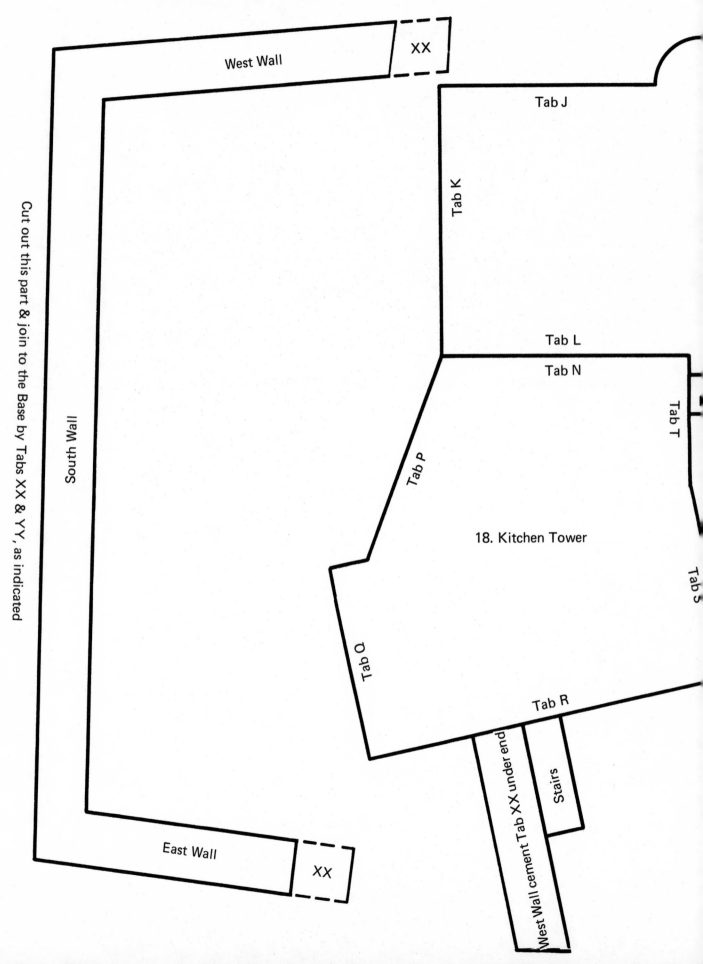

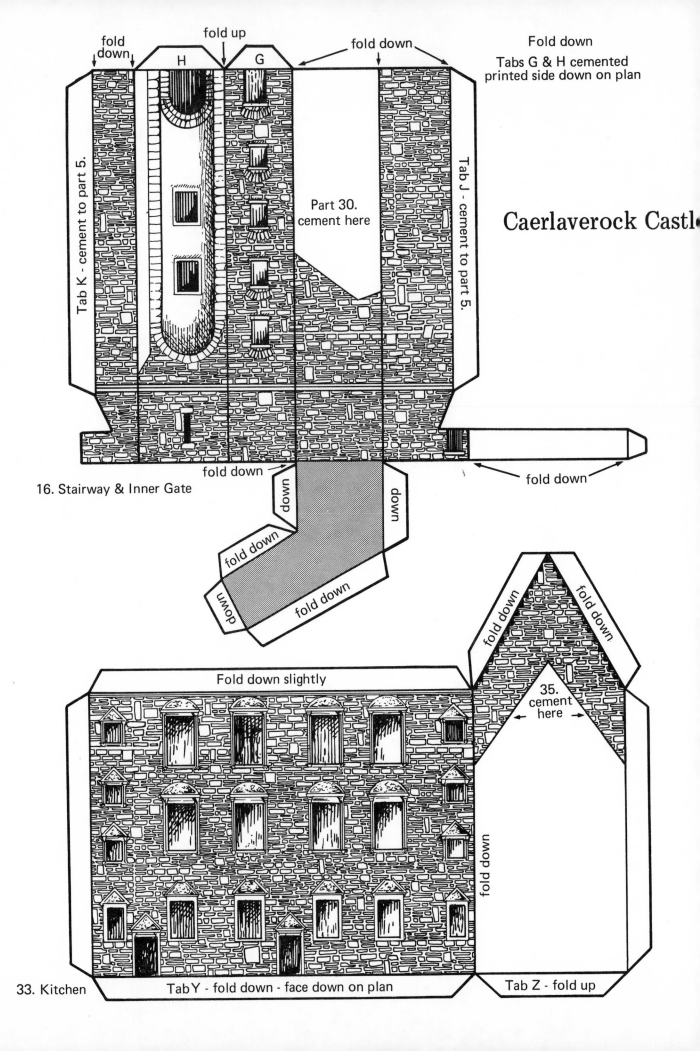

fold
down

fold up

H G

fold down

Fold down
Tabs G & H cemented
printed side down on plan

Tab K - cement to part 5.

Part 30.
cement here

Tab J - cement to part 5.

Caerlaverock Castle

fold down

16. Stairway & Inner Gate

fold down

down

fold down

down

fold down

down

Fold down slightly

fold down

fold down

35.
cement
here

fold down

33. Kitchen

Tab Y - fold down - face down on plan

Tab Z - fold up

Caerlaverock Castle

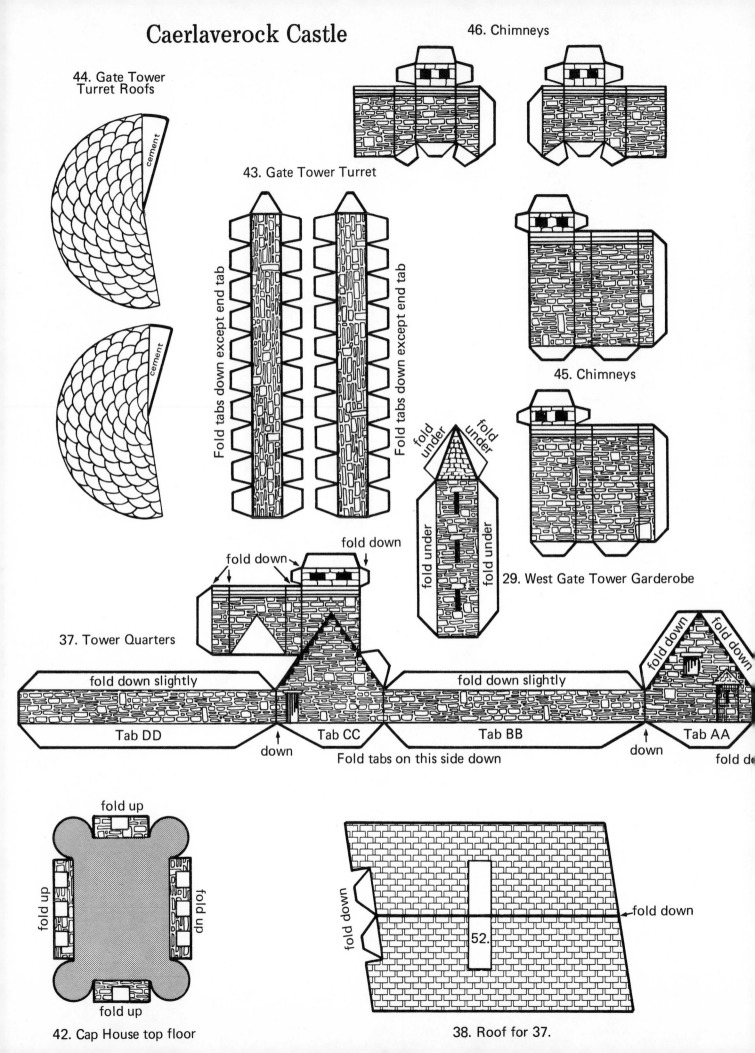

44. Gate Tower Turret Roofs

cement

cement

46. Chimneys

43. Gate Tower Turret

Fold tabs down except end tab

Fold tabs down except end tab

fold under   fold under

fold under   fold under

45. Chimneys

29. West Gate Tower Garderobe

fold down

fold down   fold down

37. Tower Quarters

fold down slightly

fold down slightly

fold down   fold down

Tab DD   Tab CC   Tab BB   Tab AA

down   down

Fold tabs on this side down   fold d

fold up

fold up   fold up

fold up

42. Cap House top floor

fold down

fold down

52.

fold down

38. Roof for 37.

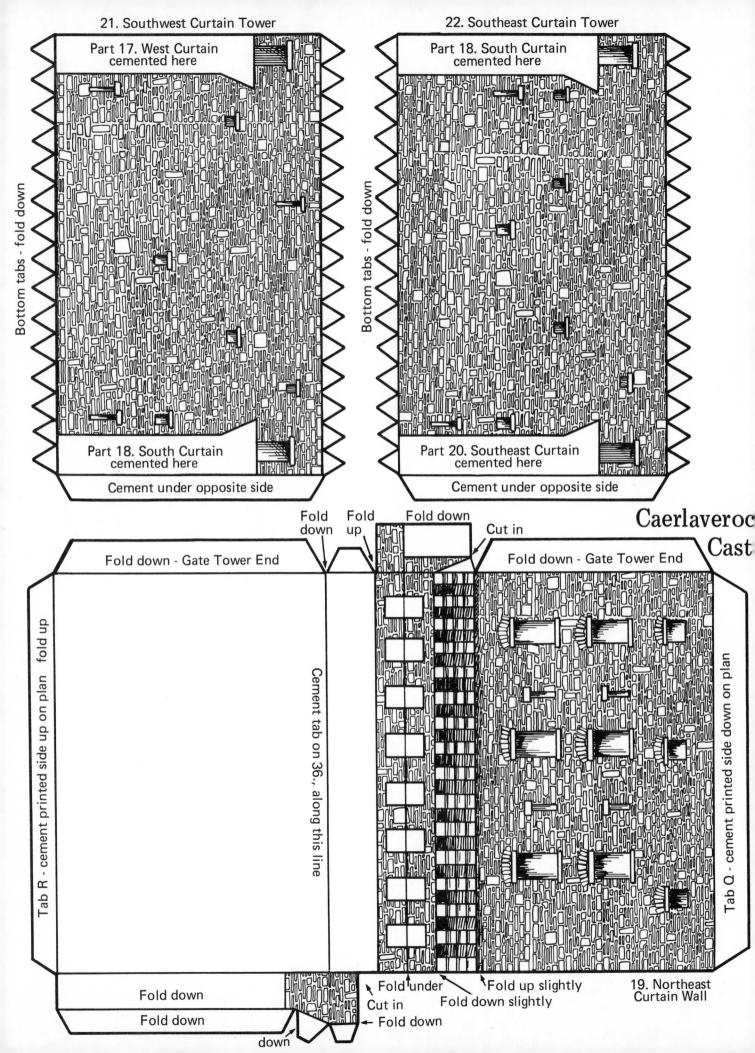

21. Southwest Curtain Tower

Part 17. West Curtain cemented here

Bottom tabs - fold down

Part 18. South Curtain cemented here

Cement under opposite side

22. Southeast Curtain Tower

Part 18. South Curtain cemented here

Bottom tabs - fold down

Part 20. Southeast Curtain cemented here

Cement under opposite side

Caerlaveroc Cast

Fold down

Fold up

Fold down

Cut in

Fold down - Gate Tower End

Fold down - Gate Tower End

fold up

Tab R - cement printed side up on plan

Cement tab on 36., along this line

Tab Q - cement printed side down on plan

Fold down

Fold down

Fold under

Cut in

Fold down

down

Fold down slightly

Fold up slightly

19. Northeast Curtain Wall

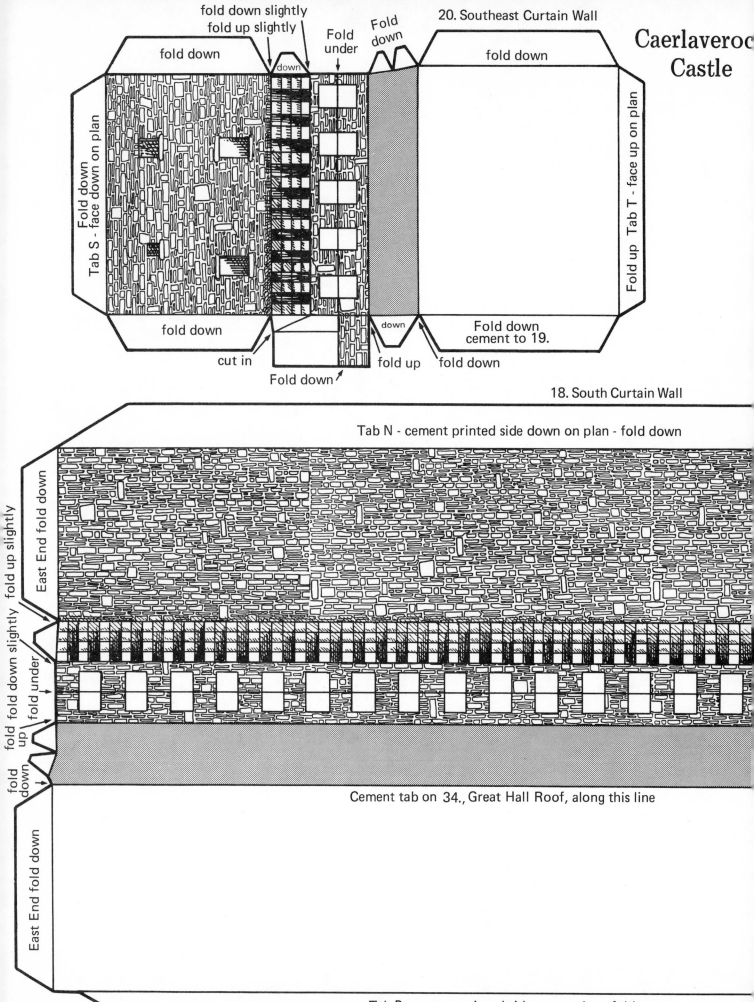

fold down slightly
fold up slightly

fold down

Fold under

Fold down

20. Southeast Curtain Wall

fold down

Caerlaveroc Castle

down

Fold down — Tab S - face down on plan

Fold up — Tab T - face up on plan

fold down

cut in

Fold down

down

fold up

fold down

Fold down cement to 19.

18. South Curtain Wall

Tab N - cement printed side down on plan - fold down

East End fold down

fold up slightly

fold down slightly

fold under

fold up

fold down

Cement tab on 34., Great Hall Roof, along this line

East End fold down

Tab P - cement printed side up on plan - fold up

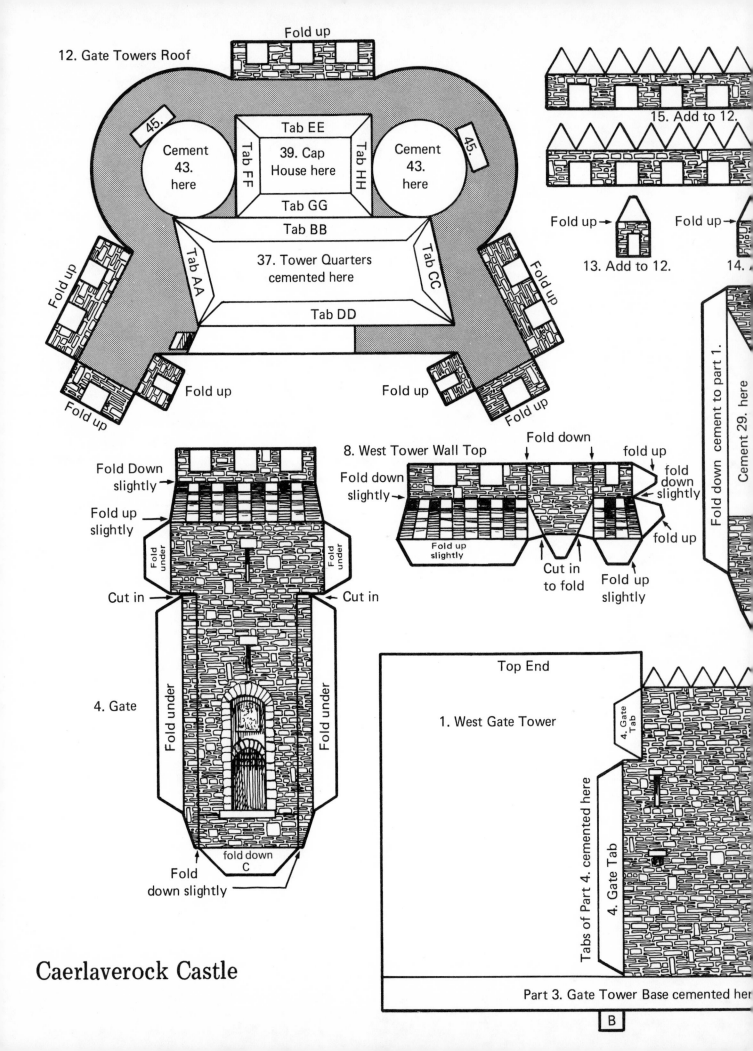

12. Gate Towers Roof

Fold up

45.

Cement 43. here

Tab EE

Tab FF

39. Cap House here

Tab HH

Cement 43. here

45.

Tab GG

Tab BB

Tab AA

37. Tower Quarters cemented here

Tab CC

Tab DD

Fold up

Fold up

Fold up

Fold up

Fold up

Fold up

Fold up

Fold up

15. Add to 12.

Fold up →

Fold up →

13. Add to 12.

14.

Fold down cement to part 1.

Cement 29. here

Fold Down slightly →

Fold up slightly →

Fold under

Fold under

Cut in →

8. West Tower Wall Top

Fold down

fold up

Fold down slightly →

fold down slightly

Fold up slightly

Cut in to fold

fold up

Fold up slightly

← Cut in

4. Gate

Fold under

Fold under

Fold under

Fold under

fold down C

Fold down slightly →

Top End

1. West Gate Tower

4. Gate Tab

Tabs of Part 4. cemented here

Gate Tab

4. Gate Tab

Caerlaverock Castle

Part 3. Gate Tower Base cemented here

B

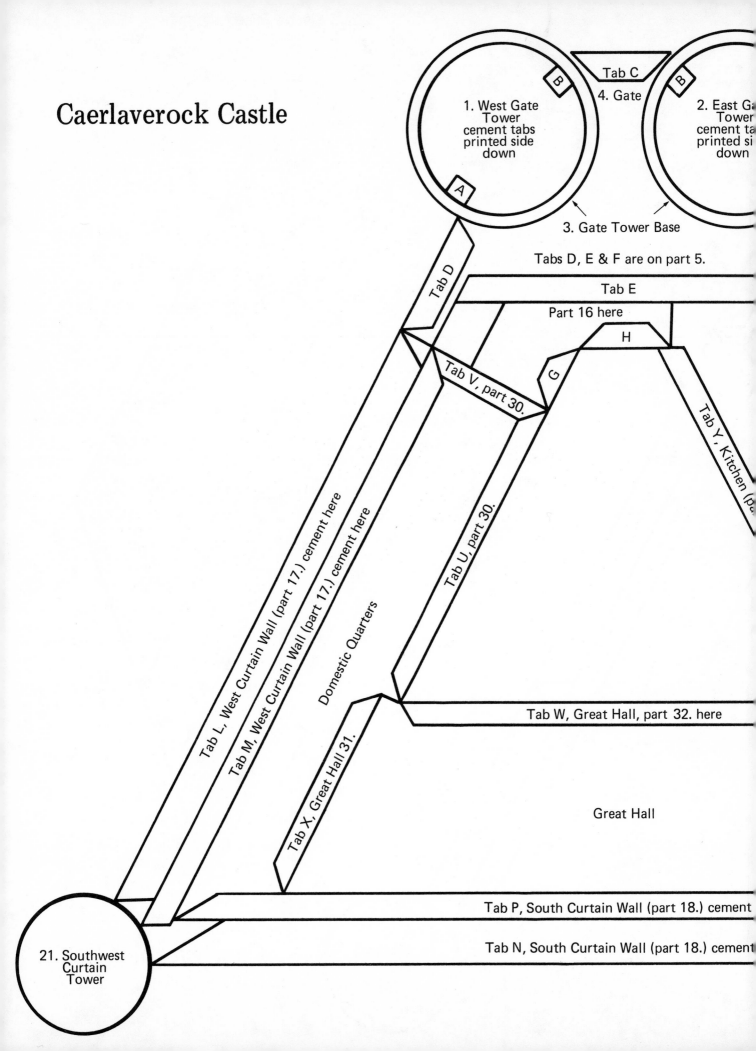

Caerlaverock Castle

1. West Gate Tower cement tabs printed side down

B

Tab C

4. Gate

2. East Gate Tower cement tabs printed side down

B

A

3. Gate Tower Base

Tabs D, E & F are on part 5.

Tab D

Tab E

Part 16 here

H

G

Tab V, part 30.

Tab Y, Kitchen (pa

Tab U, part 30.

Tab L, West Curtain Wall (part 17.) cement here

Tab M, West Curtain Wall (part 17.) cement here

Domestic Quarters

Tab X, Great Hall 31.

Tab W, Great Hall, part 32. here

Great Hall

Tab P, South Curtain Wall (part 18.) cement

Tab N, South Curtain Wall (part 18.) cement

21. Southwest Curtain Tower

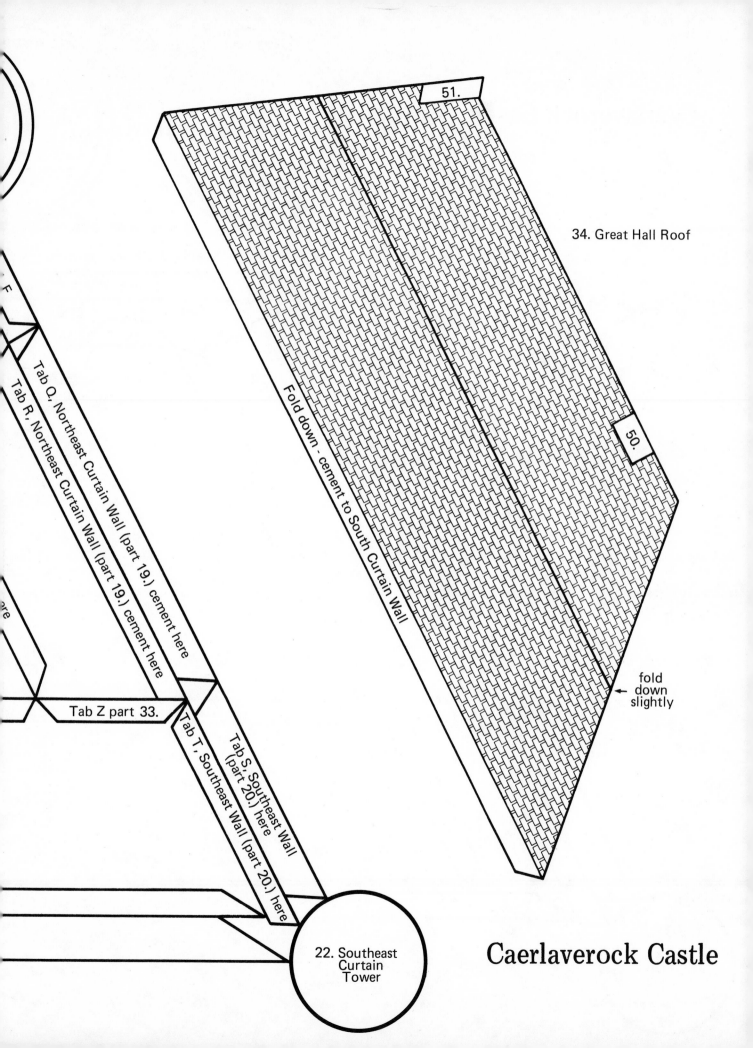

51.

34. Great Hall Roof

50.

fold down slightly

Fold down - cement to South Curtain Wall

Tab Q. Northeast Curtain Wall (part 19.) cement here

Tab R. Northeast Curtain Wall (part 19.) cement here

Tab Z part 33.

Tab S. Southeast Wall (part 20.) here

Tab T. Southeast Wall (part 20.) here

22. Southeast Curtain Tower

Caerlaverock Castle

Caerlaverock Castle

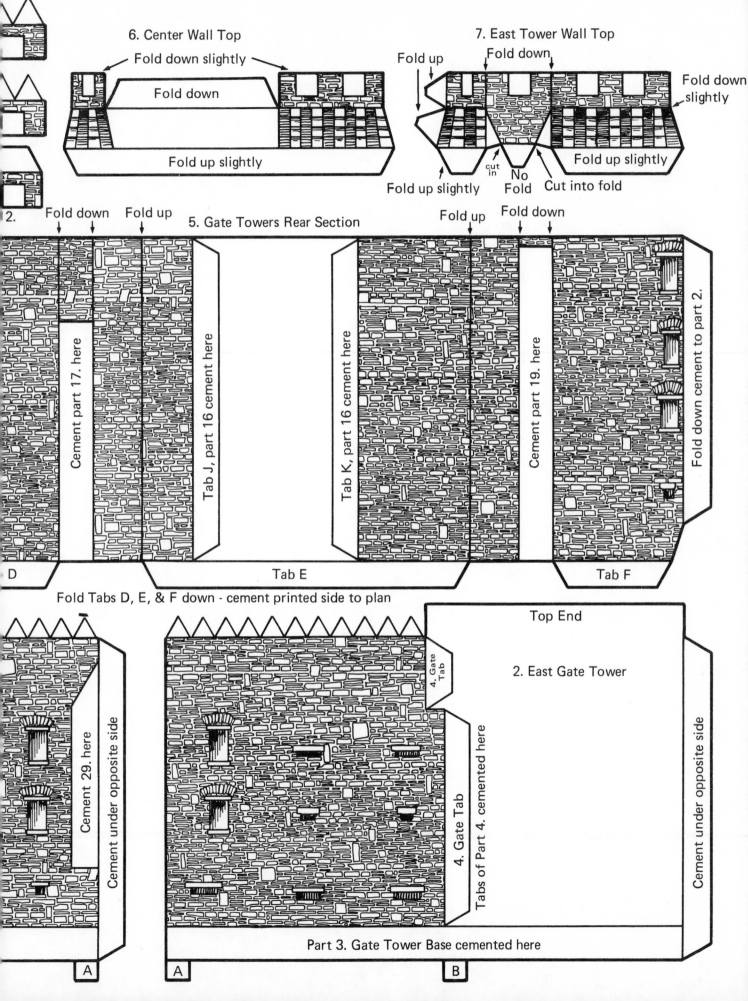

6. Center Wall Top

Fold down slightly

Fold down

Fold up slightly

7. East Tower Wall Top

Fold up

Fold down

Fold down slightly

Fold up slightly

cut in

No Fold

Cut into fold

2.

Fold down   Fold up

5. Gate Towers Rear Section

Fold up   Fold down

D

Cement part 17. here

Tab J, part 16 cement here

Tab K, part 16 cement here

Cement part 19. here

Fold down cement to part 2.

Tab E

Tab F

Fold Tabs D, E, & F down - cement printed side to plan

Cement 29. here

Cement under opposite side

4. Gate Tab

Tabs of Part 4. cemented here

Top End

4. Gate Tab

2. East Gate Tower

Cement under opposite side

A

A

B

Part 3. Gate Tower Base cemented here

Caerlaverock Castle

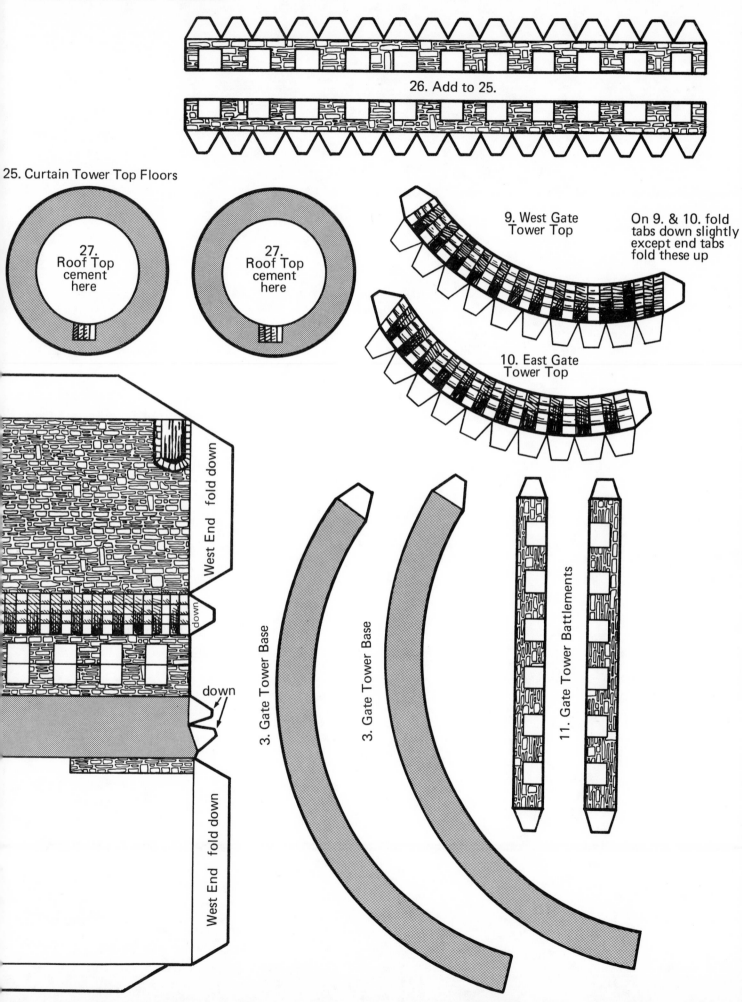

26. Add to 25.

25. Curtain Tower Top Floors

27. Roof Top cement here

27. Roof Top cement here

9. West Gate Tower Top

On 9. & 10. fold tabs down slightly except end tabs fold these up

10. East Gate Tower Top

West End fold down

down

down

West End fold down

3. Gate Tower Base

3. Gate Tower Base

11. Gate Tower Battlements

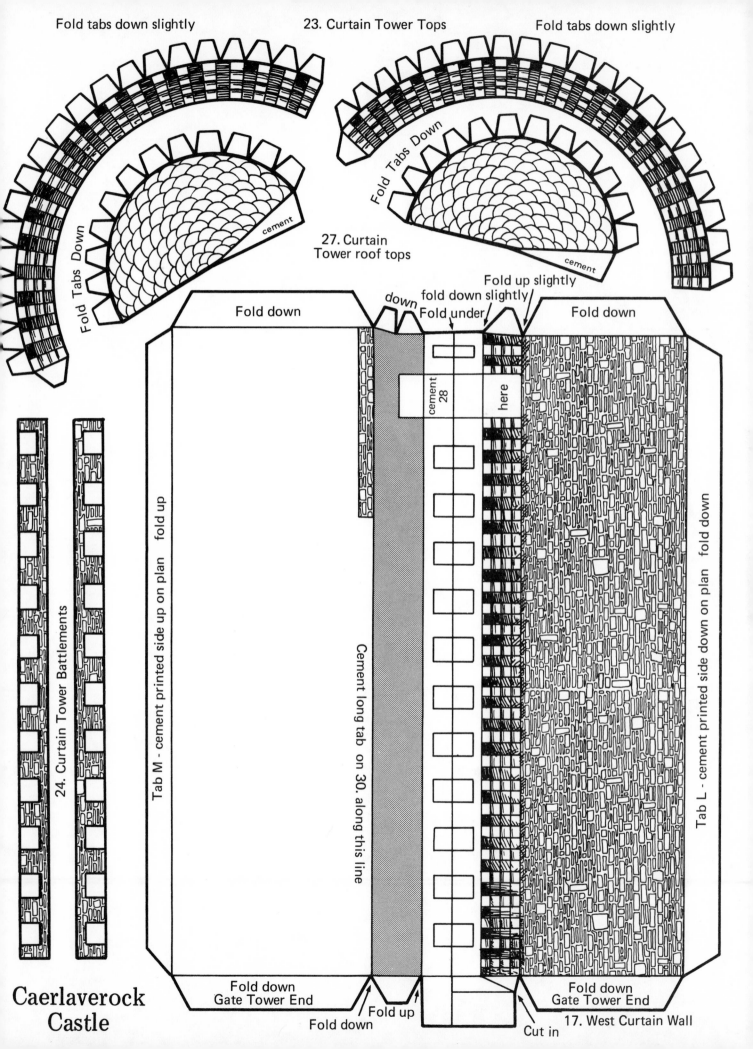

Fold tabs down slightly

23. Curtain Tower Tops

Fold tabs down slightly

Fold Tabs Down

Fold Tabs Down

cement

cement

27. Curtain
Tower roof tops

down

Fold down

Fold up slightly
fold down slightly
Fold under

Fold down

cement
28

here

Tab M - cement printed side up on plan   fold up

Cement long tab on 30. along this line

Tab L - cement printed side down on plan   fold down

24. Curtain Tower Battlements

Caerlaverock
Castle

Fold down
Gate Tower End

Fold down
Fold up

Fold down
Gate Tower End

17. West Curtain Wall

Cut in

Caerlaverock Castle

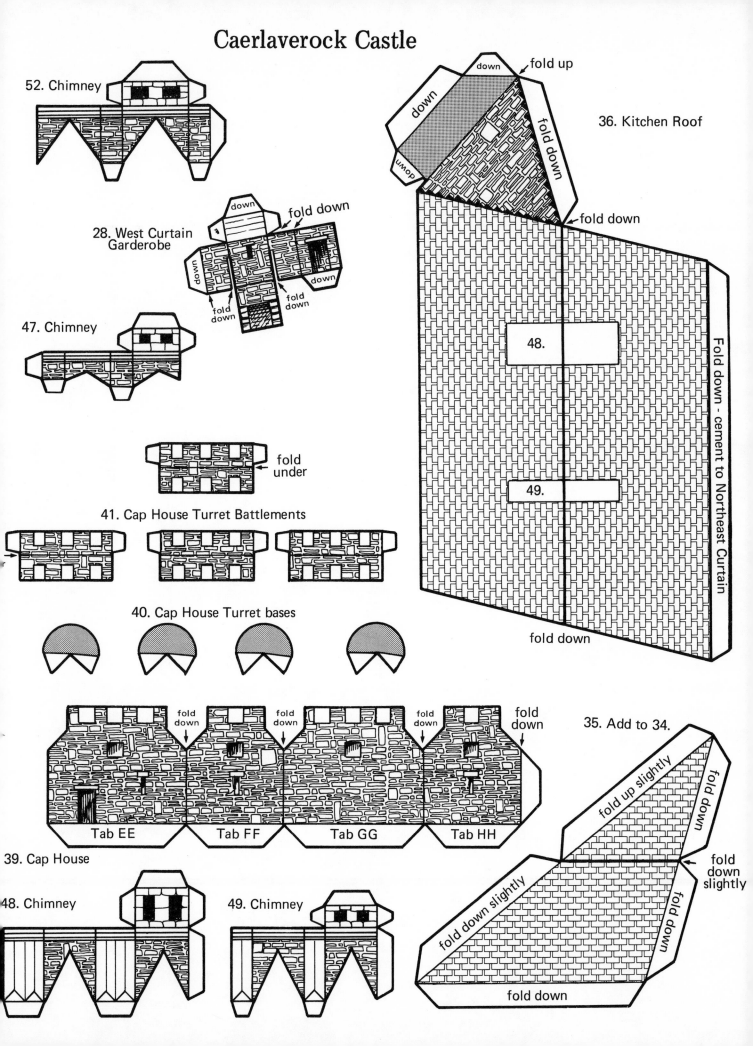

52. Chimney

28. West Curtain Garderobe

fold down

down

umop

down

fold down

fold down

47. Chimney

fold under

41. Cap House Turret Battlements

40. Cap House Turret bases

Tab EE   Tab FF   Tab GG   Tab HH

39. Cap House

fold down   fold down   fold down   fold down

48. Chimney   49. Chimney

36. Kitchen Roof

down   fold up

down

umop

fold down

fold down

48.

49.

Fold down - cement to Northeast Curtain

fold down

35. Add to 34.

fold up slightly

fold down

fold down slightly

fold down slightly

fold down

fold down slightly

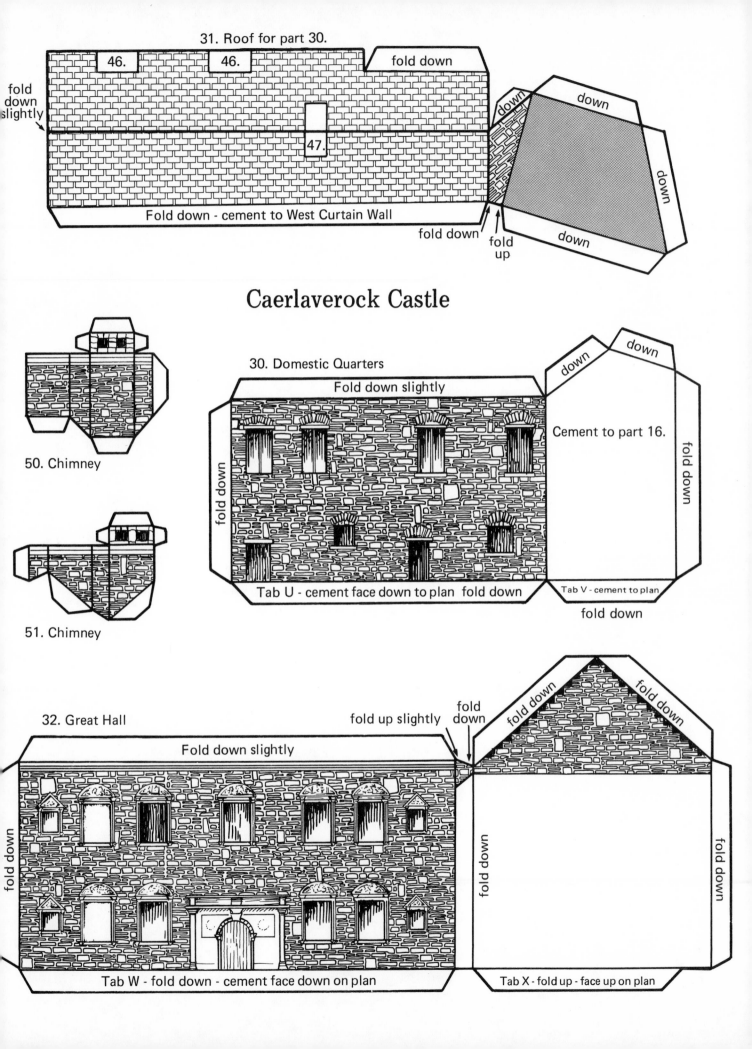

31. Roof for part 30.

46. 46.

fold down

fold
down
slightly

down

down

down

47.

down

Fold down - cement to West Curtain Wall

fold down

fold
up

down

Caerlaverock Castle

50. Chimney

51. Chimney

30. Domestic Quarters

Fold down slightly

down

down

Cement to part 16.

fold down

fold down

Tab U - cement face down to plan   fold down

Tab V - cement to plan

fold down

32. Great Hall

Fold down slightly

fold up slightly

fold
down

fold down

fold down

fold down

fold down

fold down

Tab W - fold down - cement face down on plan

Tab X - fold up - face up on plan

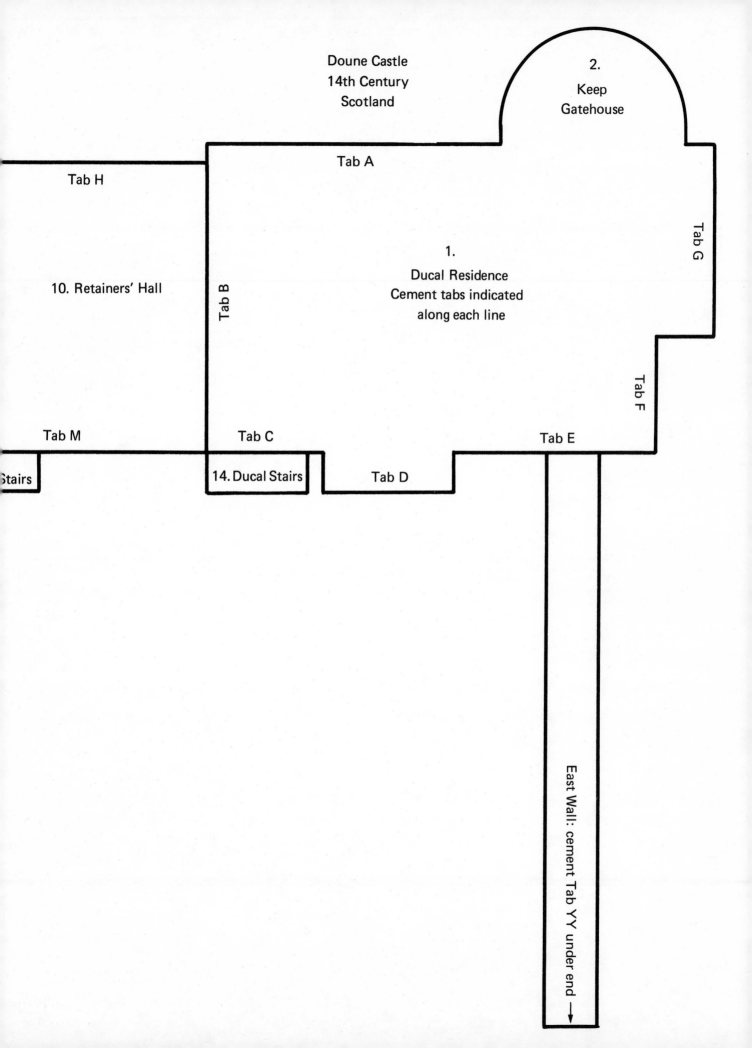

Doune Castle
14th Century
Scotland

Tab A

Tab H

Tab G

10. Retainers' Hall

Tab B

1.
Ducal Residence
Cement tabs indicated
along each line

Tab F

Tab M

Tab C

Tab E

Stairs

14. Ducal Stairs

Tab D

2.
Keep
Gatehouse

East Wall: cement Tab YY under end

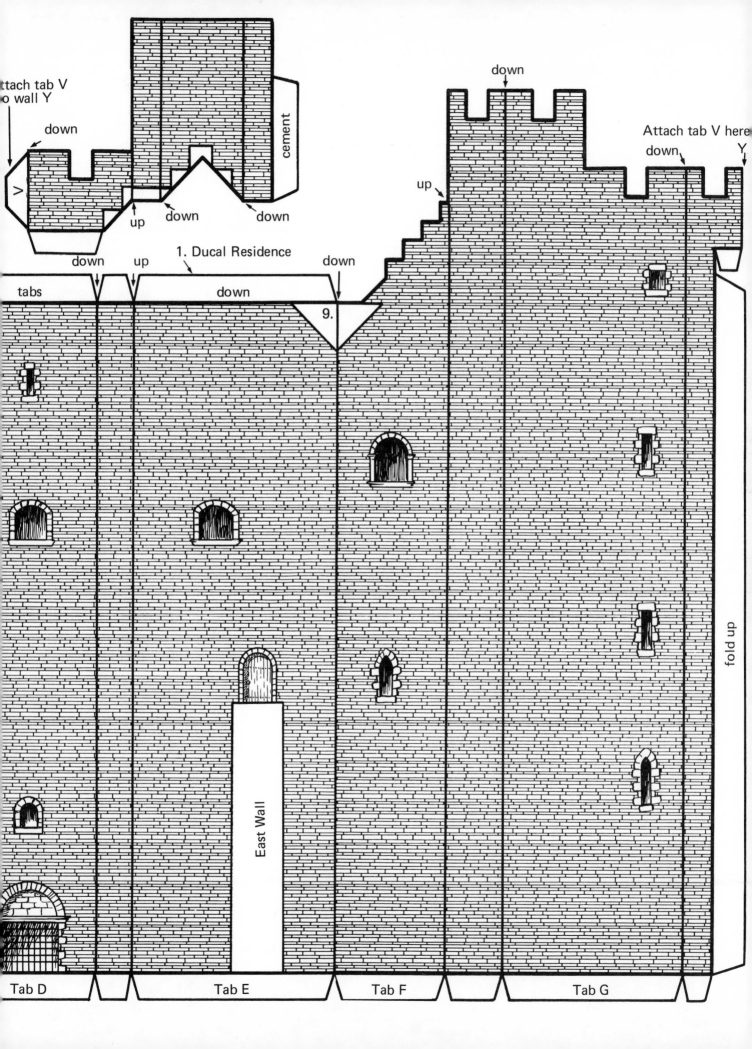

Attach tab V to wall Y

down

V

cement

down   down

up

1. Ducal Residence

down   up

tabs

down

down

9.

down

up

down

Attach tab V here

down   Y

East Wall

fold up

Tab D   Tab E   Tab F   Tab G

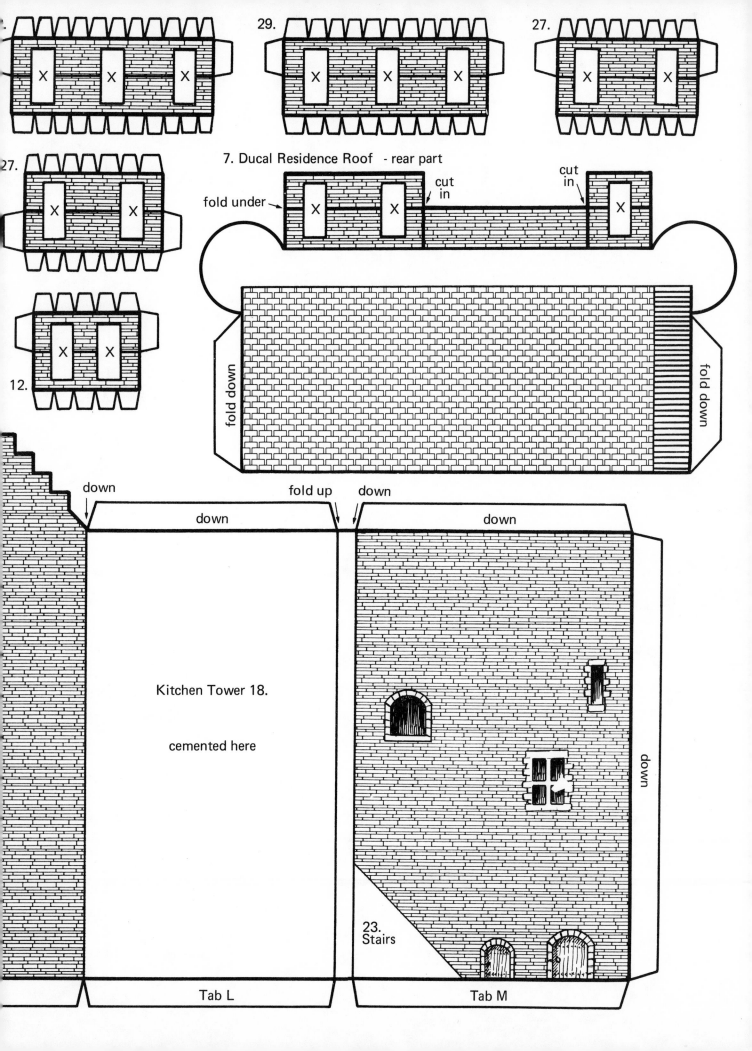

29.

27.

27.

7. Ducal Residence Roof - rear part

fold under →

cut in

cut in

fold down

fold down

12.

down

fold up down

down down

Kitchen Tower 18.

cemented here

down

23.
Stairs

Tab L Tab M

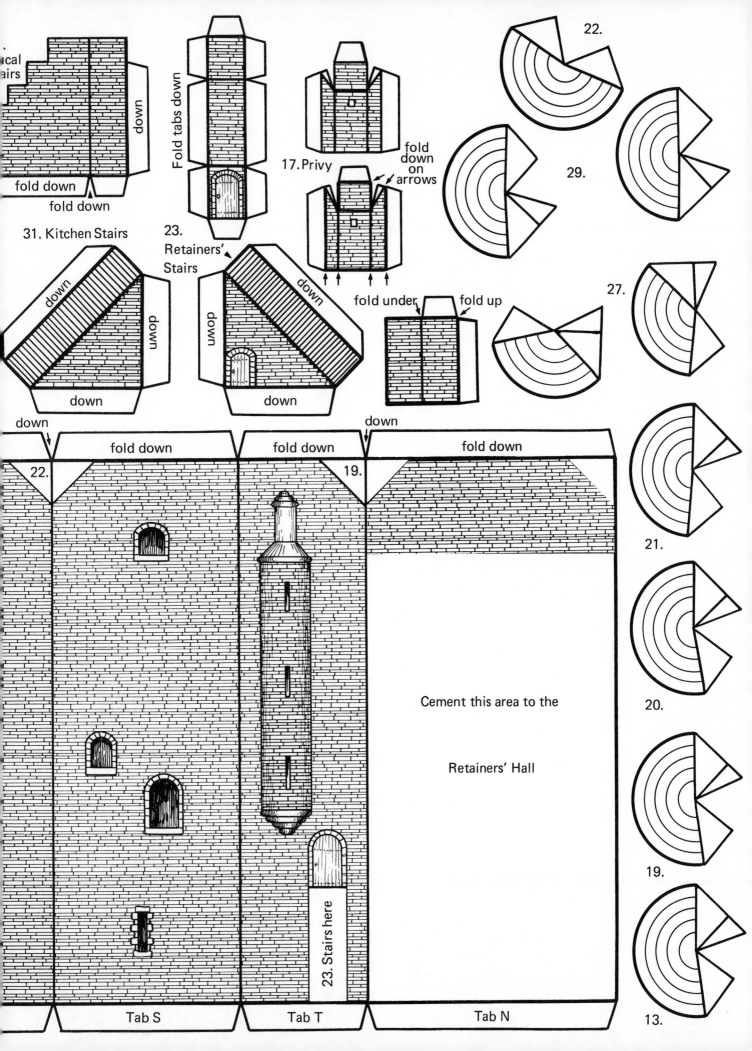

ical
airs

fold down

Fold tabs down

down

fold down

fold down

31. Kitchen Stairs

23.
Retainers'
Stairs

down

down

down

down

down

down

down

down

17. Privy

fold
down
on
arrows

fold under   fold up

22.

29.

27.

21.

20.

19.

13.

down   fold down   down   fold down   down   fold down

22.   19.

Cement this area to the

Retainers' Hall

23. Stairs here

Stairs here

Tab S   Tab T   Tab N

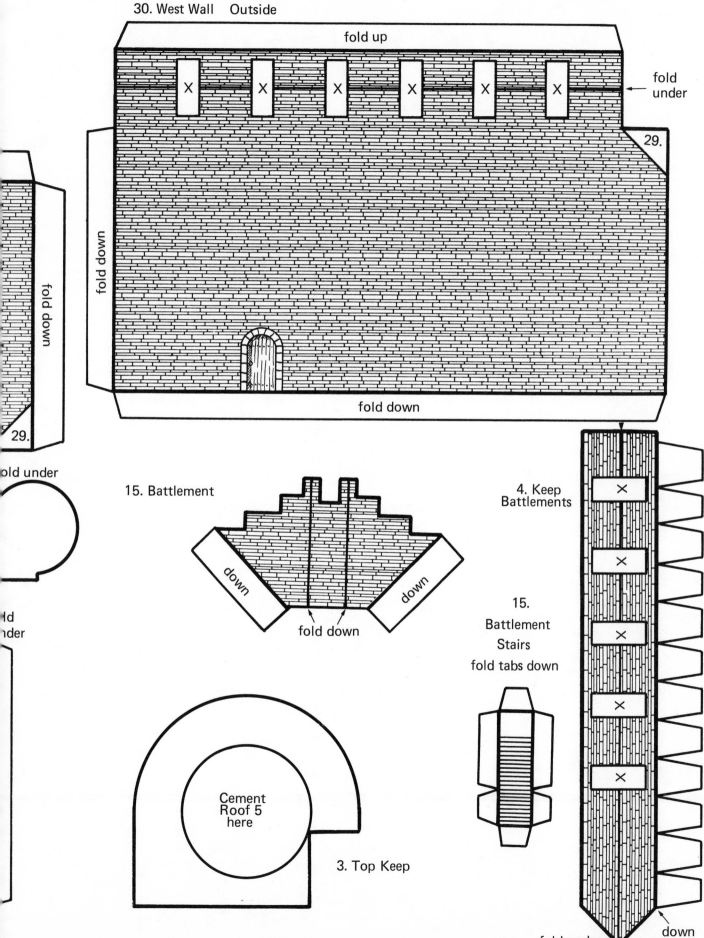

30. West Wall   Outside

fold up

X   X   X   X   X   X

fold under

29.

fold down

fold down

fold down

29.

old under

ld nder

15. Battlement

down   down

fold down

4. Keep Battlements

15. Battlement Stairs

fold tabs down

X

X

X

X

X

Cement Roof 5 here

3. Top Keep

down

fold under

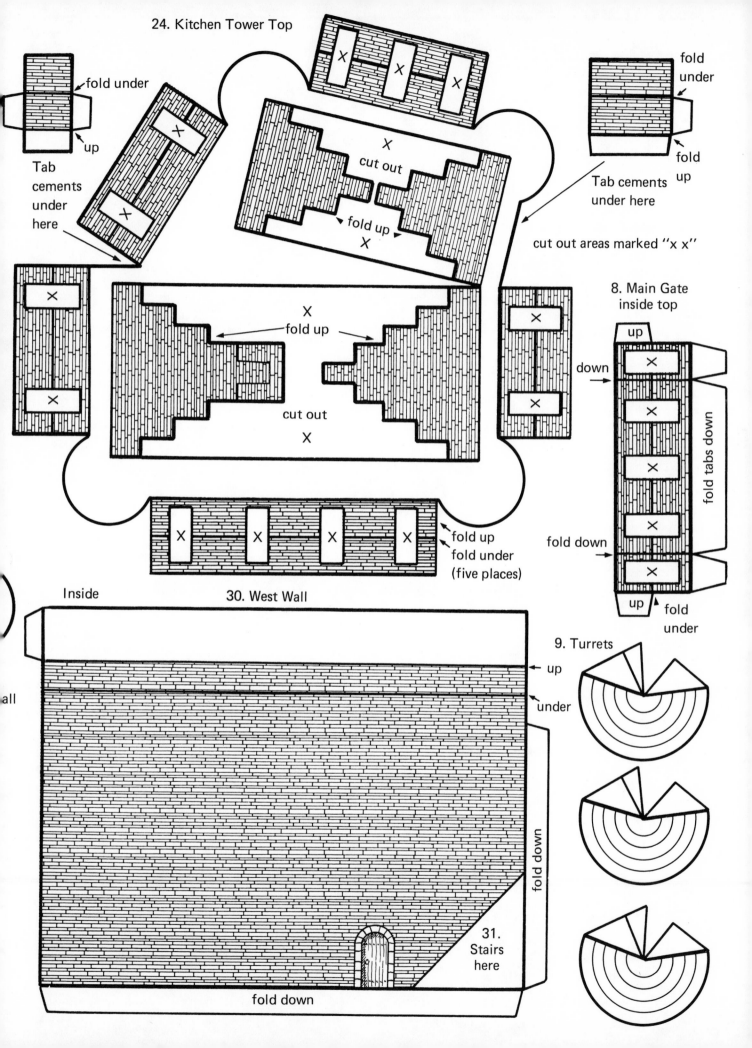

24. Kitchen Tower Top

fold under

up

Tab
cements
under
here

cut out

X

fold up
X

X
fold up

cut out
X

Tab cements
under here

cut out areas marked "x x"

8. Main Gate
inside top

fold under

fold
up

up

down

fold down

fold tabs down

fold under

up

X
X
X
X
X

fold up
fold under
(five places)

X   X   X   X

Inside

30. West Wall

up

under

9. Turrets

all

fold down

31.
Stairs
here

fold down

CAERLAVEROCK CASTLE

Caerlaverock, the "Lark's Castle," stands on marshy level ground where the River Nith flows into the Solway. The name "Solway" comes from the *"Sul Wath"* or "Muddy Ford" across which ran one of the main routes connecting the West Marches of England and Scotland, and Caerlaverock Castle was an important place during the Scottish wars of independence and the troubled times that followed.

The castle is first mentioned in October 1299, when the English, profiting by their victory over Sir William Wallace at Falkirk, had placed a garrison in the fortress of Lochmaben, a few miles away. Sir Robert Felton, the commander, reported to King Edward I of England that "There is a castle nearby called Caerlaverock, which every day has done and continues to do great damage to the King's castle and his people." But Felton added that he had just killed Sir Robert Cunningham, the Constable of Caerlaverock, and fixed his head to the battlements of Lochmaben.

Next year, Edward in person led a powerful army through the West Marches and laid siege to Caerlaverock. His stone-throwing mangonels forced the garrison to submit after a brief but gallant defence, during which they inflicted sharp losses in men and horses upon the English. The story of the siege is told in a poem, written in French, which lists the coats of arms of more than eighty knights bannerets who commanded troops of cavalry in the English army, and also describes the castle itself —

"Shaped like a shield it was in form"

that is, triangular, with a tower at each corner. Of these towers, one was double, with the gate, approached by a drawbridge, below it; and round about were ditches filled with water. The walls and towers of the castle that can be seen today fit this description very well, but are a hundred years or more later than King Edward's time, and it is possible that in 1300 the castle did not occupy the present site but stood about two hundred yards away, where there are foundations that seem to belong to an older fortress.

Caerlaverock was recovered by the Scots in 1306, when Robert the Bruce, after killing the Red Comyn, asserted his claim to the throne and placed himself at the head of the patriotic cause. But the castle was soon again in English hands, and in 1312 the Keeper of Caerlaverock, Sir Eustace Maxwell, was still numbered among the supporters of King Edward II of England. He changed sides soon afterwards, and the castle was razed to the ground in accordance with Bruce's policy of destroying all strongholds that might give shelter to English garrisons.

During the fourteenth century the power of the Maxwells continued to grow. Caerlaverock was rebuilt, and again destroyed, and once more rebuilt. Our model shows the castle that was begun early in the fifteenth century and altered and improved over the next two hundred years.

This castle was begun soon after the building of Doune, and its plan reflects the same theory of defence — that is, in both castles the main gate, where the strongest attacks were expected, was made the strongest part of the fortifications. Earlier castles, like the Tower of London or Château Gaillard, had had great donjons, or, as they were later called, keeps, protected by outer defences, where the garrison might make a last-stand when the outworks had been captured. But the strength of the donjon was often wasted; if the outworks were held, the donjon was not needed, and if they fell the garrison usually gave up anyway.

However, the fortifications of Caerlaverock were more advanced than those of Doune in several respects. The towers were crowned with machicolations — that is, the battlements were carried on stone corbels projecting from the face of the wall, with wide gaps in between through which heavy stones, quicklime, or the traditional boiling oil and molten lead could be dropped on the heads of attackers who succeeded in crossing the water-filled moat and reaching the wall's foot. Moreover, the fortifications of Caerlaverock were improved later in the fifteenth century, and again at the start of the sixteenth. Gunloops, or, as we usually call them, loopholes, pierced through the walls of the towers, reflect the increased importance of firearms. Through them, the defenders could direct crossfire, so that the towers could protect each other as well as the curtain walls between them.

Caerlaverock is most easily approached from the north, and the gatehouse faces in this direction. A drawbridge led over the moat — now largely filled in — to an arched entrance between two round towers, fifty-two feet high from the surface of the moat to the bottom of the corbels that carried the machicolation. The towers themselves and the gatehouse behind them were built in the early fifteenth century, but the gateway arch, which joins the towers and gatehouse into a single block, was added about fifty years later, and in the sixteenth century the inner end of the gateway passage was strengthened, so that the gatehouse could be closed off from the courtyard inside the castle and held if enemies forced their way in from the rear. After these improvements, the passage could be blocked from the outside by an iron yett, or gate fashioned of interlacing bars, like the one that still survives at Doune. Behind this was a portcullis, controlled from an upper chamber above the new entrance arch, and then a second portcullis, in the original part of the gatehouse, and finally a third portcullis, part of the defences on the courtyard side. On the ground floor of each tower was a guardroom, and there were three upper floors in each tower, whose rooms provided living accommodation as well as access to the gunloops guarding the gate. These upper rooms were not reached directly from the guard rooms, but by spiral stone staircases on each side of the courtyard front. These are part of the early sixteenth-century additions; before this time there may have been wooden steps in the same places.

Above the middle of the gatehouse block rose a two-storied square "cap-house" with small turrets at its corners. We have given it a flat roof, and imagine sentinels standing on it, looking out not only northwards but, since the gatehouse is higher than the southern defences, over the Solway sands and towards the English border.

> They watch to hear the blood-hound baying;
> They watch to hear the war-horn braying;
> To see St. George's red cross streaming;
> To see the midnight beacon gleaming;
> They watch against Southern force and guile.

Behind the gatehouse, two curtain walls, seven feet thick at ground level and nearly five near the top, and originally probably about fifty feet high, run back to the south-east and south-west. They are 111 feet long, and ended in two round towers which were linked by a third curtain, 137 feet long. The south-western tower is still well preserved, and is known as "Murdoch's Tower," because the unfortunate Duke of Albany, the lord of Doune, was imprisoned in it before his execution in 1425.

The triangular courtyard was probably always crowded with living quarters for the lord's family and the garrison, built against the inside of the surrounding walls. However, the castle's domestic buildings were remodelled much more drastically than its defences. The row of buildings along the west side of the court seems to date from the late fifteenth century, but the buildings on the south and east are of the early seventeenth century. The handsome carved stonework above the doors and windows shows how the influence of the Renaissance was making itself felt even in the troubled Marches, where law and order were not yet fully established. The wide windows and fine chimneys, leading up from handsome fireplaces in the principal apartments, reflect new standards of comfort; and the whole shows the wealth and pride of the Maxwells of the time. This pride is also shown in a carved panel above the gate, where the arms of Robert Lord Maxwell, who became Earl of Nithsdale in 1620, are displayed along with those of Scotland, and of Robert's ancestors, the Earls of Mar and Morton. His motto, is carved on a scroll at the bottom of the panel, and welcomes visitors to the castle.

Of the new domestic buildings, the most important, but now the most ruined, was the Great Hall, which occupied the eastern half of the south range, and was entered from the court through a handsome arched doorway whose classical architecture again bears witness to the influence of the Renaissance. West of the Hall was a large "withdrawing-room," to which the lord and his family could retire for privacy after they had presided for as long as they thought necessary over the feasting of their retainers and soldiers.

Next the Hall, on the ground floor of the east range, was a scullery, communicating with a large kitchen, beyond which was the bakery. In the bakery was a well — the water that surrounded the castle would have been undrinkable even by our ancestors' standards, because the "garderobes" or privies, of which there were several in the gatehouse block and one on the west rampart walk, discharge directly into the moat.

Above the kitchen, there were two upper floors, providing more living accommodations.

The Maxwells of the late sixteenth and early seventeenth centuries lived wilder and more dangerous lives than one would have guessed from their fine buildings. At the time of the Reformation, they held to the Roman Catholic faith, and so were on the losing side in the troubles that led to the defeat of Mary Queen of Scots and her flight to England. After her death in 1588, when the defeated Spanish Armada had rounded the north of Scotland and was making its way homeward down the west coast of the British Isles, it was rumoured that the Lord Maxwell of the day was in league with the Spaniards and that a Spanish landing in the Solway would follow. King James VI took the threat seriously enough to march into the south-west with an army, secure the Maxwell castles, and imprison their lord.

The situation was complicated by a feud between the Maxwells and another great family, the Johnstones of Annandale. Johnstones and Maxwells harried each other's lands, burned each other's houses and lifted each other's cattle. The king was quite unable to keep the peace, but kept up a show of authority by naming as his Warden of the Western March the head of whichever family seemed to be winning at the moment. So in 1592 Lord Maxwell was back in the king's favour and employing two hundred men in strengthening his castle of Caerlaverock while he destroyed the Johnstone strongholds. At the head of two thousand men — his own retainers and those of the Lairds of Lag and Drumlanrig, who had suffered at the hands of the Johnstones — he attacked the tower of Lockerbie, which was defended by its formidable lady.

A small force of Johnstones came to the rescue, but took to their heels when they saw the great force of the enemy. The Maxwells and their friends gave chase, without putting their forces in order — and suddenly found they had fallen into a trap. Johnstone had kept most of his men hidden, and charged down on the Maxwells, who were driven back into Lockerbie in confusion. Here Lord Maxwell himself, an old man, "tall and heavy in armour," was beaten to the ground. He stretched out his hand for mercy, but Johnstone struck it off, because Maxwell had offered a reward to anyone who brought him Johnstone's head or hand. His friends ran away —

> Adieu Drumlanrig! false wert aye
> And Closeburn in a band!
> The Laird of Lag, frae my father that fled
> When the Johnstone struck off his hand!

What happened next is not certain; but one story has it that the Johnstones went on chasing their enemies, and the Lady of Lockerbie came out of her tower to see how the fight had gone, with her great iron keys at her girdle. There lay her enemy, bleeding and defenceless, and she used the keys that he had demanded from her only a few hours before to beat his brains out.

continued

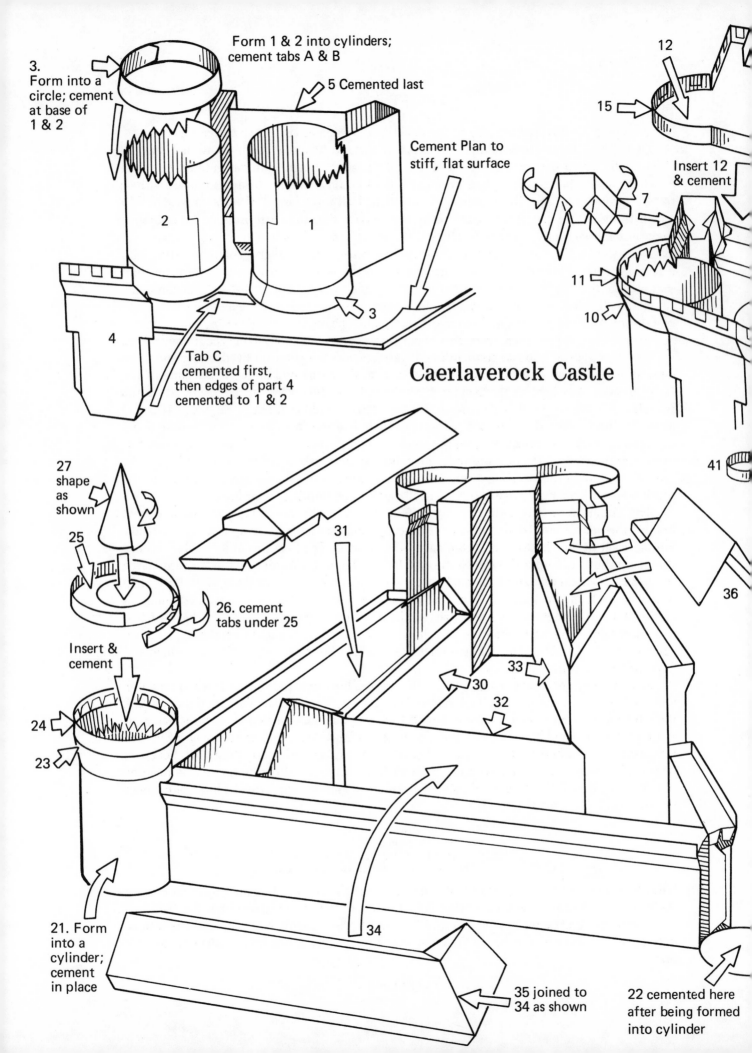

3.
Form into a circle; cement at base of 1 & 2

Form 1 & 2 into cylinders; cement tabs A & B

5 Cemented last

Cement Plan to stiff, flat surface

2

1

4

3

Tab C cemented first, then edges of part 4 cemented to 1 & 2

12

15

Insert 12 & cement

7

11

10

Caerlaverock Castle

27 shape as shown

25

26. cement tabs under 25

Insert & cement

24

23

31

30

33

32

36

41

21. Form into a cylinder; cement in place

34

35 joined to 34 as shown

22 cemented here after being formed into cylinder

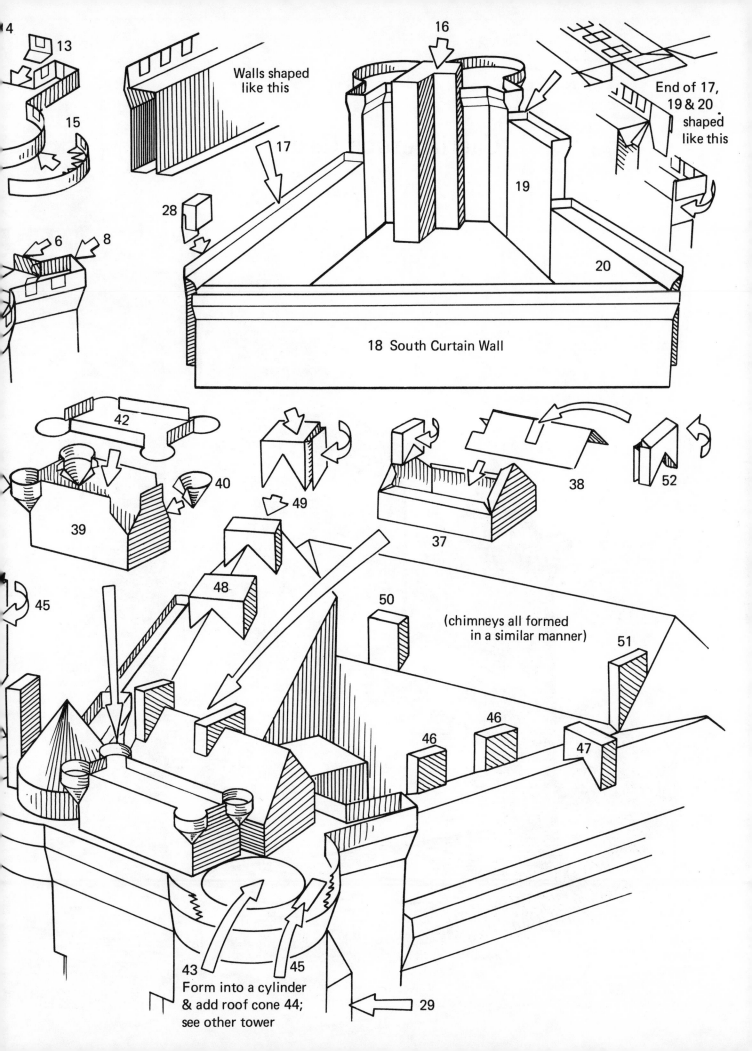

4

13

15

6 **8**

28

16

Walls shaped like this

17

19

20

End of 17, 19 & 20 shaped like this

18 South Curtain Wall

42

40

39

49

38

37

52

45

48

50

(chimneys all formed in a similar manner)

51

46

46

47

43 45

Form into a cylinder & add roof cone 44; see other tower

29

Caerlaverock Castle

Johnstone was of course outlawed; but, since he had shown that the Maxwells could not "keep the peace of the border-side," within two years he was himself appointed Warden, his chief qualifications being twenty murders, committed before he was thirty and in England as well as Scotland. The feud dragged on, and in 1607 King James, by this time King of England as well as Scotland, arranged for a meeting between the heads of the two factions. But instead of making peace the new Lord Maxwell struck Johnstone down and bade defiance to his enemies —

> Though I hae slain the Lord Johnstone
> What care I for their feid?
> My noble mind does still incline
> He was my father's deid.

But times were altered: King James from London could "govern Scotland with his pen better than his ancestors had done with the sword," and Maxwell went into exile

> Adieu! Dumfries my proper place,
> But and Caerlaverock fair!

Six years later he returned to Scotland, was caught, and hanged in the Grassmarket of Edinburgh. But his estates passed to his younger brother, "fair Robert of Orchardstane," who carved above the gates of Caerlaverock the coats of arms that have already been mentioned. Lord Nithsdale (as he was created in 1620) repaid the favour that had been shown him by taking the side of King James's son, Charles I, when in 1639 the King with an English army marched against Scotland in order to put down the Solemn League and Covenant.

In 1640 Caerlaverock stood its last siege and held out for three months against the Covenanters. It may have been after this that the south-east tower and most of the south curtain were demolished, so that the castle was no longer defensible. It was perhaps still habitable down to 1715, when the last Earl of Nithsdale joined the Earls of Kenmure and Derwentwater in their attempt to place King James VIII, the grandson of Charles I, on the throne instead of the Elector of Hanover, better known as King George I.

Nithsdale was captured and condemned to death when the Jacobite army was destroyed at Preston. King George refused to grant mercy, even though Lady Nithsdale caught hold of the hem of his coat; he dragged her across the room before he could shake her off. But the lady still had one trick to play. The night before the execution, she visited her husband's prison in the Tower of London, with a party of other Jacobite ladies, to bid the prisoner farewell. None of the warders noticed that one more lady left the Tower than went into it; for in the midst of the party was Nithsdale himself, wearing his wife's long cloak and hood.

King George's comment when he heard the news was that Nithsdale had done the best for himself that a man in his position could do. One wonders whether he had after all had some notion of what was going to happen, and the warders had been told not to count too carefully.